Flat Front

Jordan Marcum

Flat Front
Copyright © 2025 Jordan Marcum

DARK THIRTY POETRY PUBLISHING
ISBN: 978-1-0685766-4-5

All Rights Reserved

Marcum, Jordan
First edition

Artwork by Mack Taylor

DTPP32

All rights are reserved. No part of this publication may be reproduced, stored in a retrieval system or transmitted in any form or by any means, electronic, mechanical, photocopying, recording or otherwise, without prior permission from the author. Neither the author nor publisher allow for this work to be used in training AI.

DARK
THIRTY
POETRY
PUBLISHING

For Sharon and Steph

How Does A Butterfly Die?

Should there be an overstated natural disaster in some mythic schedule of what will occur to all us living folk: Lay the flowers at the bending of my arm, into the readiness of my hands, and do not ask me questions, please.
I won't be remembered for enduring the seasonal depressions swelling and deflating over the course of my life
And I refuse to be known for the times in which I didn't carry myself with senses of propriety or the unspoken Vow of silence accepted by those who did not love me or wish me well in the true reality of the life we'd lived
Not with any animosity, it's just something else. I don't want a reward for participation. It will not be my hand cradling yours or your back on the way to and from Alicante, Spain - Neither one of us paid for that excursion.
It will not be me that knows I was in fact truly cherished during my lifespan; and I will die as the butterfly did.
Of old and young age in tandem. I will be obliged to learn these social languages all over again - It will not be
me who makes these fruitful mishaps, mistakes, ego parades, flights of fury. I want the flowers I got in trouble for picking when I was a child.

Rheumatism

I put the thing
In a lunch bag
In an envelope
In a brand new
Absence of something to hold onto
An intangible artifact made of mud
That licks away blemishes and ruin
Soon to be sold
Soon to be held
How did I invent such an ugly thing
Passed down by
Digs or darlings
I never knew it could happen to me
I never thought
Thoughtfully in
The imagination I used to possess
But here it goes
I have to use an unnatural habit to
Fight the fight
I'd looked for
And deal with bad dreams and new
Painstakings
Pin, meet needle; I think you two'll
Find harmony
In every young, old, woman's body
And I'll deal with the joy and regret
Punctured in
Some days I

Find it funny
I laugh without moving my mouth
An insect girl
Had no ideas
And what a transition it was to go
From foam wings and a flat chest
To a garment
Abomination
To fresh meat
Hooks and slabs of me equivalent
To your new
Clothing strung out, pinned to wire
Calling back for the wind as it dries
What if I go dry?
I do not know how to dream about
Anything new
Anything else

Half Dried Clay

Tell me what you know of the spotless condition of the floor in the sauna. Does this condition overrun the fun in your fear of being found out? You look at me laughing as you sweat it and you look, to me, like a kid once again.
We are two friends. We discuss our nipple bruises, how those came about or what time in which they did, bumps on furniture, carpet marks on our ankles caused by our sitting on our feet and leaning in. We clock how lost men look when they go down South. Our books are still under our beds, yet to be read with complete attention paid to them. I scrub to and fro on the tiles, bouncing the brush, shaking gunk that was here before my parents were, off. You say I've lost weight in my neck; I know, and I'm quite proud of it. I wish to count the rubber ducks glued to your dashboard once more, but I am somewhere else; talking to you over the phone is quite difficult.
Regardless, our faces are misshapen artifacts, varnished toys, glossy sweaty messes. I loved to hear your talk on those nights of swimming and clay and alcohol and the smell of those things. I forgot, for a while, about being undesirable to
people. I called you my friend. I call you my friend. I don't have any intention of tarnishing my memory of you.

Chelsea

Tuxedo dog, below the back porch wooden bench seat
Poking his little head out from under where I'm sitting
One he hears my father turn on the hose to water a fern
I Think It Is
In the shell ceramic pot tucked at a ninety degree angle
Though it's labored, time to breathe, those instant need
Pingings in the wilderness of my mind and what buried
Things I find each time I get out of it and into the lakes
Civilization
I am safe wherever I am from now on; I will risk more
By doing nothing with what is limited to this one body
I Know It Is
Imperative I understand as much as I can while able to
I will call my doctor tomorrow morning, and ask them
If there is anything I can take for the withdrawals I am
Having; I am the opposite of ashamed of my bad habit
I'm recovering, and doing it ahead of what is expected
For A Girl
Who was so lost or ran into scary monsters on her way
Home, a swooning glowy pure glistening sky traveling
Left despite the breeze blowing in all directions and to
No Where
I am safe intensifying my focus writing this passage to
Myself and those who may remember me as I am dead
Staying stock still, one leg up and one eye on the rocks
And Birds
And Dogs
As they play around in grasses as dancing pretty things

Often do, never minding the gaps in the fences or their
Unconscious momentarily expressed pangs; finally the
Palms above radio thin and tall as a million matchstick
Pieces columns needles joints posts towers or supports
I'm wanting the radio again, to hear it echo and ping a
Sweet one into the raucous headlight frank summer air
Sweet Air
I used to envy people on planes until I started traveling
And I still have no passport, and have not left America
Though I'd like to. In fact, I think it would do me good
I should leave my backyard, kitchen, my bathroom, too
First Thing
In the morning, when I will attain all my life's bearings
Once my day comes to a close, I will hand them to you
Surely you can figure out what activity to do with them

Sand Angels

I dip my middle finger into the eye socket of the salty shore, and as I twirl counterclockwise in the midday frenzy
of nature flirting with the supernatural, I hear the song of the railroads, the crossroads, the greyhounds barking and burning fuel into an exhausted body of space in the divot of a seat of the beach bright and not brittly hot so that it blinds and binds and sticks to the spooling spirals of sand gatekeeping the uncircumcised elements; spotted, halfway unsatisfied. The distant dead eyed horizon raises its volume of liquid whispering levitating as the compression keeps coming; unseparate from the rest of us, let down inside the feral spring. My father was stationed here; he kept a box of hats and buried it in 1991. The idea is stale. The sand is stale. It quit its split. It doesn't think enough to move. It doesn't want a semblance of a thing to do with the sky that taunts it for being so small and fine. Bloated clouds hang as they'd always thought of hanging like, umbrellas stand until they don't; the wind giving in to the shrapnel edge of fearful living, mounting it, seeking inglorious lateness and stillness after being laid to rest in a body unsure of what it wants to be. Form born in requiem torn shorts, weeks away and unpacked.
Bloated clouds burst and now there is forgetting. The contact falls to pieces; clams dance because they're afraid of the rain. I'm in the furthest reach of the shell,

sleeping on dioxide smoking the admission that dies with you and I and the ambient ocean.

Drinking From the Infamous Pond

Pickup ingeniously constructed, for
Chunks of envy chucked by Dennis
Spatter over
I will never get away from that idiot
Idiot I loved and did not admit to it
Cut peach slices on the windshields
Swiped away
To and from around the barn's bend
He asked if I'd lick his plates clean,
I agreed to it
Every other, afternoon, after school,
Such a suspect time, a youthful bird
Chirping and feeding on the remnant
His hard shell gave way to my beek
Bickering back at bread being fed to
A starved feathered liar laying there

Fried tomatoes, musical chairs lover
Baby, she was just such a lovely one
Too bad. She fried her temporal lobe
Fried green tomato brained tiny babe

I lick all those plates clean, any one
They ask me to do my special work
On and on and, like a dancing mom
Overworked, unwillingly employed

Like a sex crime of passion witness
I'm a little older, oh I look different
Than I did since my son came back

We're arrogant traits, adopt none of
Us; the barley navel barrels, cannot
Go to the fair, this season; this year
Here we go about the way the goats
Bleat and believe in the nothings of
The wilds; blessed you who dawdle

She was last seen wearing a brown
Romantic neckline maxi dress and
Daisies scattered through satin hair
And her name was Rosebud Everly
She had no teeth and little dignities
Upon a tarp lifted. Soot rubbed off.
What have you gathered from this?

How so? How soon will this heal?
I drink because what else will I do
When the fruits fall off the thread
And you say I'm a damaged good

A Primordial Phenomenon That Is Connecting and Disconnecting With You at the Same Time

I do not sleep enough to meet you in the astral realm
But if my body is pressed against your body
And we breathe in the same cadence
And our palms kiss the way I've always wanted to try
Holy palmers kiss, that type of romantic shit
Maybe I could meet you in our dream space
And cultivate stronger manifestations for the love I'd
Like to give to you and make you aware of over time
I am seeing you in less than twelve hours and holding
You in my mind already in a month, you've not left it
And my jaw is tight because that's my door
And you, pressed against it; your weight blocking the
Thoughts from fleeing, and I am afraid of you leaving
I'm also afraid of you pulling me into you
But being afraid is what doesn't make either of us feel
Good, and all we want to do is to feel good
We're free to feel good as we all do believe we should
We make eachother laugh/come/stay, keep saying nice
Things, who knows what will fill this slate?
I just know I'm not going to fuck things up
Did you see the full moon? Did you dream of faces in
Her shaping the wave, crashing on our shared cadence
Stumble over the stalking moonfaced moonbeam word

Dust shines and lingers; for the most we barter eternity
Is linked to the rind; I know you're gonna slip by soon
And I'll let you, because in your words, "It's all love",
And that is certainly way to put it, albeit a bit general.
I keep thinking, maybe I made a lot of this up and the
Word of desire, or shape of desire, is simply a project.
Life is an experience of testing irrevocable limitation.

White Bellied Cat

The other night in my room
Don't inquire when that was
Yes, yes, I am an insomniac
I asked Stella as she purred on my stomach as it pointed
to the ceiling with that damned smoke alarm
If she thought I was a good person or an above average
person, at least a little
I was seeking and I'm still seeking her notes on the
knowledge of life and what she'd do another way
If she was truly living mine
I kept as still as I could just so she'd stay on my faux fur
covered acid a bag heaving entrapped stress
Hi pine tree scent litter box
I watched her behave in the kitchen like newly occupied
parents watch a tiny toddler walk into ocean
The ocean that welcomes them and seashells at the
bottom are now eggs and ham and pasta and meat
She whacked her tail on the back of my head whilst
sitting on the black plastic coffee maker, brewer!
She's tapped it on this page
Placed her outstretched paw into the marked depression
in my palm, her purr then a daggy projection
Of the quiet perfection felt
In an otherwise terrifically scary predatory city, shovel
lung window stoop tourist trapped clutch hell
She bit my knuckle as I feared and feared and feared
and feared and feared and feared how I was not
Near enough able to please

The woman I love, I do not think I will be able to love
anyone else nearly this much, in this intensity
I'd looked up from a study
Of a mid-century, feminist, legendary, Victoria Library
honored, controversially debatable authoress
And I saw Stella had left the door of my food and
sustenance womb with haste and went to the door
And I loved her little purrs
But she needed to roam and scratch the walls and scour
the space for her own sustenance, preferring
Tuna, and hubris had for it
But I hold her in mornings
Each week I model her business, her art pieces, her
experiments with texture and breaking skin with
Furious feline curiosity, thin redded lines on the back
on my pale dry palms, convex of life's mittens
Marks from play - dates, times, place, evidences of
individualistic yet domestically twined existence
Yesterday she rubbed her left ear, the one with the scar
on the side, on the side of my glowing laptop
Chased Black Beetle Bug out of my room once it flew off
my desktop, and headed into her kitchen's
Unslept misguided sunlight
I followed into the common area and watched as she
drank from the kitchen sink faucet, the gurgling
Of pigeons across from the window scoring the scene,
spilling in with a call for her attention, yet one
Of the pigeons, there were three total that morning, flew
West to the Hudson, and Stella stared as the
Other two pigeons slept in.

The Stationary Ripple Effect

Trick true, sit, wait, dog-eyed
Picky wondering wit why and when and how what has been has been and what is gonna be
Purple suede jacket guy of my dreams, in his arms the child I left behind, it seems
I'm one of those witches, baby
Ruined sleep of desperate time
More than enough for the table to share, to eat as a last resort for a meal, as a last meal, to see the look on another's face as new developments occur with it
Teresa has some nieces who conjure up prophecies about as often in increments as I do, my grandmother's sister, the one who won't dive out in nights
Holes in the mesh made of holes
Chainlink lips telling off the spits
I'm in more than a place at a time
Moving around in around yet still
Stuck on a little corner on a couch
Radiator clicking with hot rain swirling, slushing, a balloon headed baroness of half asleep central heating
We're all becoming infants; movement is the only way to be happy and strong, the older generation is more infantile and the younger generation is more productive sociologically, so the world is anew forevermore; that is what all the worlds do
Father, come into the room and visit and see what I'm working on
I did it for you

I do it for you
Father, while mother is sleeping, help me restore the wedding photo of her parents cutting into their cake
I left the vacuum out in case
Are you as confused about astral projection and the activity of enlightenment and the stew of these undeniable truths as I am?
Bronze diffuser, elephant music box, energizer home cameras, a vase made of whatever the fuck that material is; is it crystal, is it something stone?
Little tiny boxes to put teeth in, baby teeth, little teeth, unsure teeth, curious teeth, all these statues are of big figures holding little figures
And then
Texas Benjamin Toast on the counter spots its predator
A little white unicorn; is that the front of the desktop, of the drawer top, of the head top, or is it the head of the house?
The head of the house is the television, the Human Resources guy. Howling, time howling at me white disjointed numbers and letters delivering themselves like steak knives to ridged friction gives, everything a portal to reports, those that I stole from streets in New York around May, those that I hid in my left asscheek pocket and named an acronym to the nearest hospital, where my heart was.
All I see in the main area, the hair writhing out the television's itchy scalp, are five hundred and fifty three individual portals.
And I am a river. The black mirror switching out now saying there is nothing but a black beacon on; ideas, a-

swelling and crashing and landing in my lungs and down in the ripples of them and the tarps in them, the holes in them and wishing and pissing and shitting and crying like an infant in them and the dusty orange fingertips on them and knee bones plunging out of them and the spit of them, and the tremulous trembling effects that being destitutely alive has.
These are only items. They weren't born from a body. If I think about it hard enough, I remember my birth well.
I hope I remember my death, and I hope to come to accept it won't always feel like I've gotten the short end due
To the hate I buried the seed of and watered with effacing indecisions.

The Two Fighters and Two Very Cold Strangers

The forever river, your stream of consciousness
What does it mean, one who seems to know all?
Picking your nose, there exists the existential cr
-isis

Number five and it is now the end of the month
So you can really truly celebrate your survivals
If you feel up to doing things like that anymore
All those who helped you through happinesses

Two men standing in 1959, a snowstorm in this
Place in New York less than a hundred miles a
Way from Canada, Seneca Lake, hanging wall
Of weathered weather, one of the men was my
Grandfather and I believe in the photograph of
Him he is seeing beyond survival, he is seeing
The possibility of his skin cells joining snows
In a frozen state of fear dancing forever in the
Winter, Henry and Tesseyman ride coattails a
Navy blue sharing secret humor immortalized
They prefer to eat the reductive on a hot plate
Who was the third man? Was he a friend or is
He the enemy; are those emancipated streaks
Of light white shooting stars cig burns or the
Snowfall on a mission to terminate with kind
Consideration and unprejudiced frostbittered

Finite spindle of chance

Two witnesses stuck in a blackened morning
Standing still for a second, smiling at the hill
Both quivering daydreaming old men already

Blow

Don't you know? Like youth, as in youth, as of youth. Id; the celestial freshness cradling the sensitivity of touch and the two sexual organs used to smell, snort, laugh through, and take in the passion of a new season of life. So soon, so packed full, so ready to know another custom. So bright, so rare, burning so hot the plastic has evaporated, and those environmental scientists said that wasn't something the weather could do. Oxygen slipping into other matters, letting it simmer as it wants to in a waterbed petri dish. I'm fascinated by the nerve of mother Earth and the zits on her back I burn the roof of my mouth with. Sticking a probe into the sun's ears. "Can you hear the fires of my heart's thumps, how they howl and pump lilac unmistaken capable blood through the satellite of consciousness?" I ask Sun's beauty, a leverage in the space time continuum; who cannot help but be looked at with a hunger for wonder by cohorts spun and spinning out, painting their fingernails, chewing teeth, blessing those below the troposphere as they look up, for they have hope another tangential happening will fly in and happen and they'll have a ball and quit playing dumb in movement and speech fueled by the manmade. Lemonade unmade, underdressing, whittled, unexpectedly searching for virtues in the form of astrological advice. Your television is a portal. Your fridge is a portal. Your father noticing you've grown too big to be held by his side is a portal. Your starstruck bedroom door is a portal. Your pillow is soft and a portal. Portal is the need to be somewhere else, to be in a different mind, to lift the head and forget about both shoulders and all that you may happen to, currently or one day, lack. Sun's successfully recovered from her surgery.

And there are flowers everywhere, all over the walls, all over the departed columns and engravings and wallpapers, moth holes, glory holes, shoe soles, pet souls, cheap souls, merciful souls, portals of a soul and souls full of portals sloppy per capita of slope, anything of a slender rope of land; messing out, just messing around, so taking what she can, when she can to achieve her right to say "I couldn't only can I actually did and continue to do, you're all fools for having thought and spoken of me in need of help." Canary pleasantness, charming earnestness of a morning fix one growing and blowing and glowing under the plump grass dew, improvising its script for the day with an honest treason; once you enjoy something so fully time isn't legitimate or wise to follow; waffle patterned eyes, gum stick teeth, crumpled sheets of paper and blotted ink, exploded pen, articulation indicating one wanting but great reserve is the death of fledgling bliss in the heavyweight portal: the ribs of odium. I want to get high and dismember how I feel about you now. Name something you have that you don't deserve. Name something that smells of discovery or name the predecessor, recovery, with red nails and curlers. Name every state across the world, and it doesn't matter if you've been in the lines or on the border. You're in it now. Senses belong to you, not the other way around.

Pride as it belongs to you, leans against wrongfulness and annihilates these airways allowing it to breathe the way you do.
Little smile, little bump a little above, little by little feeling littler, littering your insides and youth has you thinking when it's done you'll look back and think how beautiful it was you chose to experience a high only to suffer and to understand the fruitful damnation of not being able to crack your back.

Divine Bounty of Woman

She was a well of acetone
And water; stones dressed, draped accessories of moss
and weeds swallowed and soaked the water at glacial
pace
And she smiled with satisfaction at her uninterrupted
and temperate cycle of absorption; a king sitting away
from
the explosive extrovert of
The world she did not possess the body to rule, yet she
ruled over the secret society of fallen, tossed pennies
and pink-kissed cigarette butts
Bygone and uninventoried
She was hungry everyday, only at 7:36 AM EST, by the
American elm where people go to practice mindfulness.
There was a simplicity to
Her nights, as there was no conceivable hunger as the
distant circle faded to gorilla hematite on evenings of
rain, were blissful and full of spontaneous, mesmerizing,
stored ideas for the poetry of the surrounded Earth,
message
and ode to the childhood of seasons innumerable, voices
distinct, and just like the sky blue color of love, hungry
always and inflated by winds that solemnly pledged to
bring ageless and faceless people out of their homes, and
to visit her with their friends, dogs, and children. On
certain cerulean afternoons, she could hear names
called to what she made out to be

A love of some immense kind; a sportsman beckoned to retrieve a ball of laughter, and to toss it over to another.

Sentinel

You know
I still think about some acts of dying
Driving the wrong way on a one way
Street
Tying into a rope my thrifted salmon
Sheet
I still am full of upset thinking how I
Must be a walking heron of horror to
Folks
Disciplined but not playing the game
Well
Sick with envy pink and green inside
Poking graphite holes through eternity
Internal organs withstanding digested
Crap

I've always thought of quitting that acting thing, that writing thing, that seductive thing, that bathing thing, that thinking thing, all of that which is not automatic. And I don't want you to know who I am unless you really liked that thing I did a few years ago. Yeah. I remember it, too. And that's also why I still act and still think and still try to lead days, never ruined and never dull, to seem poignant and thematically pungent. Because maybe someone'll notice. Just because you've told a story doesn't mean it's understood, just because I make mistakes doesn't mean I'm helpless to a generational curse. I fight resentment with my knuckles. I bury my face into the stories of others.

I have begun to see the greater world and I am absent from knowing I have a place. But I hope you know you do.

I drink by myself more than I do any other thing. Most things vary; the same activity means it the same not entirely, not full as a vending machine in the sweltering pride full summer awakening your dominion. School's out until the fall.

At least I'm yet younger; skin not flab, life not drag, hot air unseen in the snow drunkenly, celestially pissing itself onto the ground of Michigan, because there was no looking up convenient or germane. Noone stretched their spine that way. Noone needing to resuscitate those moments, though misplacing wit good prize for kids of my generation at the end of the rainbow in winter's charade game. Lighthead, he has not come with the car. Smooth Face Inferred confided in you for the temporary softness and you know it and she savors making you know it. I'm mad as a juicer, and I'm built like one, too; blades and all if you need that service. Not only could I, would I, can I suck and blow; I don't own a juicer but I've seen such pictures. Lighthead, we're going up this year; it's our turn to catch the motion.

Cut. May I? Breast reductions have left it to the starchy winds of Idaho to pick up home and delete the feeling from that coordinate, from that cordiality thing. Over and out, beats per minute on the boardwalk skyrocketing in flaring blaring exaggerated blows, flashes of iridescent light, unphased by the homeland of the moon and her children, lay -ing beside the stars, reaching for them in the current unfolding ripples of clues used for finding what home means to them; the unmet and unheard of cousin of survivor's guilt. One of the immense choices in this life thing is taped to your forehead and mine together, vibrating in a world of buzz, suffering from martyrdom, thickening red screen, still teaching a false lesson, false mythology: The choice of turning away from what you see happening; and nature is not done with us yet. We never let up on her, repaid her in special treatments and maintenance for being a creator and a destroyer of the ecosystem of inextricable evolutionary efforts sustaining life as it severs a portion from view.

Forecast says skies tonight are set to be filled in line with clouds, some territory blocked off and captured for an anticipated and continuous blood panic. I sit in the seed of myself, limbs pulled, snapped, broiled, as hip as pork tenderloin, slow-roasted, unable to return to the raw, rewinded, reminisced, reminded. I sit in my soul ditch hell, expecting the onslaught of mistakes on the projector and the diagram of how successful the financial, directorial, skin tight debut was, the shapeshifting ticking bomb slutshaming itself; each closing and opening and closing of sound a distinct epitaph. It will never leave my mind. Pouring chemicals down the hatch and rubbing the seed til it bleeds isn't the cure for this unwellness. As I've said before, the head is the problem, but I do not know if that statement was the wisest. It sounds a little ungrateful to me. If it weren't for you in the way of yourself, would it have been easier to get what you deeply wanted, like a child craving sugar the same way an insect does? Is it the truth you were once a maggot? Where were you when my first earth mother died, and here were you when, first, grandfather died with his sexism and smoke. Where were you when Carrie died, where were all your friends, the friends that love you so dearly? Hm? Is that your natural hair color? Did you give thanks, wandering far, without taking a little cream off the top? Did you see the way that nightbird looked at you? Is this night the final salvation you, o Great Lakes impersonator, have to stand still through like a stoic towering creature in a sandstorm bending backward.

This is what you get for misunderstanding prayer, praying, communicating indirectly, diminishing, diminishing.

Do you mean to treat yourself like a dusty old rug? Do you call yourself white trash? Do you believe there's too many of you? I do. I wish you'd rot with the other cowards. Do you think you're as pathetic as I accept you are?

Yes, I say to myself in the fetal position, knees bent as a folded recycling compartment, elbows bent with a trust expeditioning again and again and finding little to like of the experience. I hate people more and more and more than I love them. I see all. I see you all. And I don't want to continue attempting anything. I am stuck here, with short term amusement all too well prepared for. It's almost like the story writes itself so I keep giving it prompts.

Both exist at the same time.

I just want to belong to life.
Bathroom perfume busted eye busted nose busted lip busty women, some reduced and blown around by the wind, some surrendering to youth. Succumbing to youth. Giving into the painted set of these other sides of the rainbow, glitter shit and caked with goop. Blow once; blow from under, get the air circulating, resuscitate. Middle of night Archie rests on the end as I lay on the other side. He lays slowly and lightly breathing like a baby and never fully closes his eyes to see the hematite medallion of his dog brain. Sasha goes back upstairs, and I think maybe of her world trade skill wearing a similar costume on the first morning of July. They're going to find you out unless you apply some more pressure to this. Maggot finger crunch, chunk of leg, ear of ear, death from above selected by a casual god the method and the execution of said method. Through sipping mortified tube, the juices of forbidden harm flush into an upward maelstrom soft at the spectacle of the inner arm; leaving something to be desired inlet.

Today & Today's Calling

Slowly, lowly pull out;
Over by the sleepy bookshelf, our family has a copy of Puzo's sensationalized research
A story indicting the color of weeping, black as black can be, on a screen, globally seen
Do you love America? Are you lost in the body of it as I am? I don't recognize my family
As beige as beige can be
We've seen these corners, these open calls, wicks alight in our rooms of naked shame
Kept from the corrupts by the corrupts, joining everyone, asking over some permission
Over and over and over a horseless carousel of feeling self-diminished then becoming
Diminished in "right" ways
Hear the whistle of friction
Sliding door thirsty for oils
Stolen away, heard as late as late can be, makeup tested, grounded in this now reality
A pitcher of wine tensions
Hear the money as a bad word in public discussion, hear the kid calling in sick, hear a
Fight for the decent treatment of all people and the dreams they hold and have held to
All mouths of infants and
Their recycled, sparkled, dreary, promising, fingerpainted by thumb and sucked on true

And tried true, innocent, unknowing, undiscouraged, undone, unwinding twirling youth.
I love you, I love your family faces, do not be mistaken that the world is for your traces
To be made in the soil and sand and in all of you that defies an assigned sex at birthed
Graciousness; be ungrateful, screw the label, when not all of us are feeling so grateful
Sure, there's this and that; this pretty image, this community, names pulled out of hats
We raise children, not only inside our customs, but within stations of our live's matters
Tracks built by god, or whoever is around us, singing out the traveling wedding songs
Jingles of the heart and words unaccepted and untaught by the study of any language
Any child is familiar with what we've learned to unlearn about here and here's eternity,
Hoping they get all these
Wants with little to no trouble, to be allowed to be out from diminishing remarks as the
Independents decide it's
The time to pull away from the promises unheard and unfinalized and unfiltered by the
Sunshine, as light can be
Shining directly into eye
As unfiltered as it can be
We lost the bet; hear my call, have we lost it yet, is this all, is this us at our best's best?

Lone Road

I waited for someone to let me merge into the right hand lane. The smell of freshly pumped gasoline filled out the circular vacuum of air between everyone's cars on the highway. I was heading West. I had never done it before. I'd stopped for gum while my tank filled but the heat smeared it and stuck it to the black bag wrapped around the pack. This trip was rough and it wasn't because of the fifteen minutes I sat waiting to merge. It was because I couldn't let go of the past. I could feel people's eyes reading the sexual and social embarrassment on my forehead, like I was a scandalous billboard at the standstill. "Have you been drinking tonight?" I'd hoped nobody would ask, especially an officer. Everything pointed West and laughed West. I wanted to shut off the engine, look over the shoulder, and tell the ocean to choke on me. I sat there, in the middle of a fight I was barely winning, and waited, still, to merge.
There was, however, entertainment to witness. There's always entertainment in the West, right? I saw a single one, a single bird, a single pale chanting goshawk, land on the hood of a cerulean Chevy Cruze, turn around, lift its tail, and squirt liquid primal blackberry paint onto the canvas of the driver side windshield. It was hilarious, and gross.
I knew I had one last chance to turn my life around. I knew I couldn't fly like that bird, shitting and leaving as I'd done in human form. It was overcast that day. I merged after the car behind the Cruze left a gap for me.

That was, nice, I guess, of them. The luggage in the eyefold of the backseat was layered and zipped with postcards and note after note detailing the past two months I'd spent squatting on the waves of grass in the outskirts of Arkansas, my piss, deliciously precious time. I was excited to age, see my body widen, feel my neck settle under bloated minds in novels, conspiring against untapped potential. I'd been giving the women I met all a different name, they'd be given a nickname behind the actual word they gave that I pretended to absorb, and they would hear my gift back.
A pseudonym that did me good. I felt good. I was good. I was tempora. I was a drifter. And there was no payoff. In studying, fucking, behaving, wandering, cooking, smoking, taking, giving, raising, challenging, conversing. I did have hopes for something beyond myself, but no one wanted to know them. I took them selfishly, and I who! What when where'd, floored it. Soured it. I went West just like all the other deadbeats did. I can't believe there's anything else to be. The human world is a cesspool. They are all going one day; way or another, rapists in a line.
Just waiting to merge. Just waiting to get what they want while the others writhe and get sick on their own shirts. Once, I dated this nature photographer. He had nice hair. He knew.
Yet he was a rapist too. He was waiting for me to cave to love him like his mother. I don't want to wait like that. Horns. Lights. There is a simplicity to it. The choreographed passages the governesses designed for us to lay on.

Hide. No one will be able to make up their minds. They do not seem to have much in their minds. I don't either. Not when I'm out in the land of the living, far from sleeping in the bed of the dying. Not when forgiveness lays before me, and my payback to it is hard-earned apathy. The scripture of the cycle of starting over, an endurance.

Running Hot

I will never know what you think or how that mind
processes what it sees and senses.
Must tell you. I don't want you to miss me; it fills me
with fever at the inauthenticity.
And I don't want you to hate me, but I'm a wildfire, and
I've got trees to burn down.

You once wore a precocious sweater
Tangled between sleeves, besmirched
Neck of infinity
No passport, no passage, no sanctity
No way through
What are you not telling us? Greener
The wiser of the father fallen funeral
There is no ghost
No no holy ghost
Poetic musings and beheaded stories
Wish glass would
Sink from the sky
Cut the Swell Off
Rituals can drag you if you dare to be
Brattish or unrested in the enactments

Give up on me, for I keep returning, a
Great annoyance
Aren't you going to give up your seat
Aren't you going to apply for that gig
Aren't you going to slice it already or

Burn with the million fires you jailed

I am here to turn loose the committee
I'm here to write this and perish away
I'm here as a rambling abortion flame

There's some trouble in these valleys
I'm raining in reverse and running to
The end of time
Running hot with all the shit I've got
Repenting for the ashes of currencies
Scars, fresh as deli meat on my thigh
Where is Earth's checkbook, and if I
Soil myself as a transaction, can this
All be done and through with, soon?

Haiku: Dragon Melon

> Bright absolving strait
> Human made soft spittle sponge
> Inspiring dreary

Haiku: Where is Love

> Fencing all the time
> Facing rare eternities
> Swept around -alone

Haiku: Deflate Truth

> My mind has bled out
> Carefully scratch my scalp
> But care not bribes me

Haiku: Boss of Me

> Way to hold your woes
> You're almost like a desk drawer
> How did you learn that

Haiku: Occupation

> You act like a bully
> I'll work for someone else soon
> I know it could work

Haiku: Bolt Cutter

> Want and need shortly
> Keep eternally blasting
> You can cut locks off

Haiku: Fingerpaint

> Move around the wet
> We may need it in crisis
> Keep it in the fridge

The Boldened Swimmer

Still in the sitting waters
Desperate expressions for bubbled foams ascending to the surface
Little is heard in actuality
School bus scissor mishap
Kicking off the ritual of gauging at weeks and months of branches
Still submerged in sixties
My mother taught me how to dive when I was the kind age of nine
She'd been a swimmer in college, and I'd dive deep as I'd manage
And now I hold the tree of life with the thought this may be a year
I can enjoy, and bask in
I made it to the egg before, maybe I could break a few more and I
Could make an omelet - something to that effect; keep on kicking
Kid
I am not at all out, but I
Am used to the currents
And that's enough, I suppose, and that's exciting, I could suppose

Aubergine's Hilarious Cousin

You know that you're brilliant
You know you can do anything
You know they all think of you
And have a part for you to play
You know many statistics, and
The statistics are in your favor
You do not have to attempt the
Attempting
The world, as you know it, is an
Open door, entirely keen on you
So why fold in
When you know you've got the
Goods for all that is good, for a
Girl like you
You are fresh
You are stinking of lemon cake
Stirring in the privilege of love
You can trip
But it's all a dance for voyeurs
You know there's no worries to
The things you want to do, and
You know I quietly hate how it
Feels to talk to you because it's
Always about you
And I never had a sister, but if
That's what this is
I'd rather be alone
Yet I'm still keen on you, for a

Spade must remain with the ol'
Diamond number
You're welcome
You're welcome
Yes, you are always welcome
Yes, indeed, you have won all
The challenges with graces to
Spare, you are so so precious
Isn't that so difficult for you?
Isn't that an immense pity for
You
Participation award recipient
Gracing us with your shining
I always come around to this
Enamored appreciation away
From the envy once believed

Flat Front

"Aiding and abetting"; I once had to say in a scene and had no idea what it meant. I assumed it was a legal phrase, but it's actually still enigmatic to me. Does aiding mean complacency, and in what way is one culpable if claiming something is true if it really is? Is this strong truth scary for the reasons it is perpetuated and completely possible?

Flat Front is the place I keep turning back to. The hard, freshly squeezed realizations for when I/you come home. The manufacturer and destroyer of the sensitive heart. The heart, not sensible. How can you stand by yourself in
the Desert Storm of being a young woman? Was my father in his time serving preparing for me? Am I discharge
honorable or dishonorably discharged from having a sound mind? Flat Front is the place behind my eyes I use as refuge to hide, to bide time, and to falsely marinate in. I cannot trust my thoughts, and releasing any truth can be quite the gamble. Should I be comfortable with losing any values? For I am not so, and yet I can't forgive any of
anything. I can do it for a moment, conversation, poem. But it's lingering. The elusive shadow. The first, and not the last figure of death beyond the pale there was and never was. I can't lie when I am unsure of what I'm saying.

The shadow of shame has dictated my life and choices. It hand feeds itself like a hungry colleague at the funeral service for decency and dignity. One is possible at a time, but not both. Pick one battle. Pick one sister over that
discarded one. No one cares what I think. I should revel in that and say and think what I must, but I am trying to
find the connective thread. Why am I just a shadow? What event in the past made me into the needle leaving an
inconsistent pattern of holes? How do I cease from going over and under? How do I feel loved in a capacity, if I do not feel at home anywhere I go? From here on out, I will tap into the steep corners of the Flat Front, and help
articulate the "issues" sing out their qualms. This is an act of service solely to myself, and it feels horrible, but I am not sane sitting with the waking dream.

I want my mother to hold me forever. I still cut but I make sure it isn't deep enough to leave scars because if I get opportunities as an actor I must have a somewhat discernible body, and it should be consistently unmarked due to this fucked up world's view of the bodies in it to begin with. I am sorry I told people I was planning to die young.
I am sorry I scared people. I am sorry I gave so much of myself to people that could never love me the way I was seeking and needing when it should have come from me,

and that's the truth hitting me the hardest and smacking
me on the neck every morning. When I sleep, my arms come up and fold over my face in case an intruder steps a distance away to behead me. I wake up with spilled water, bedside and beside me. This is a dream and nightmare, for the record. That makes loss feel less cerebrally challenging. I am undiagnosed and it bothers me to no end. To tell the ultimate truth, I feel repulsive. I hate writing "I" in anything because it feels self indulgent, but I am pain; personified, it seems like. If I could offer any unsolicited advice, it would be to hold onto every drip of happiness that rains from the swirling airs of matter. - Cling to the spontaneous, take accountability, and do not dare to hide.

I first touched myself when I was five. I hate my body. I hate people looking at my body. I'm inept at making an income. I want to run away but I'm afraid I won't survive. I have made many mistakes. I've also been mistreated.
I am my parents' daughter. I cannot find a happy medium. I have the eyes of my grandmother Sharon and I have
the beautiful curse of blue eyes. I unsettle myself. It feels like there's no way out of this hell and there never was.

Oblivion is a word. That is true. What does oblivion mean to you? _____

I spent years in the company of friends and absentminded lovers, nude often. I hate being naked but crave it, too.

Poetry can be lighthearted, uplifting, hilarious, insightful, and whatever else. I hope you find it within yourself to break cycles and be content. I needed to create this collection, to write it out and be read. I've learned, practicing
any sort of martial or mental or spiritual art, to prepare for war or train as the war is actively happening, is not an effective form of self-protection. There is no self, and when we try to make ourselves separate, everyone's gonna
suffer and experience anguish. There is only so much we can do when we are sick, and all that lives is because of unbridled love and generous support. I will, one day, maybe not today, but hopefully the matters of time alive, not value the bare minimum when it comes to how I think. As I formed sentences and expressed thought in this book
I felt unintelligent, terrified, exhilarated, and doubtful. I have had to berate doubt. "Get your things and go, fucker.
You have not served me well with your actions, and I believe we need to progress in our lives with severance.", -
I say to every formation of images and memories flashing and superimposing over what I've witnessed in nights

alone and not alone.

I went to the MET a few months ago, and I saw a statue of Medea. I immediately recognized her as a mirror, for it is a great conflict, the self and misery. I think, for me, it's going to take a very long time to undo the craft of a misery I have come to know exists. Separation is a gift. Separating yourself from miseries is liberating and also a myth, or perhaps I am simply a weak person. The hilarious thing about this poem is that I'm an actor, and it's taught me to use misery in work. I don't have to stand still and smile and suck dicks. (Although sometimes you
have to figuratively do it, but for the most part, connections happen organically, and the bonds created are truly, intrinsically, and spiritually incomparable. I have never known so many beautiful people, and I didn't think I'd
be able to. Ultimately, I think what I've been struggling to say is that I'm hopeful for things to change. Change and hope are a divine combination. In The Other Side of Venus, a character based from hopes I had at 17, spoke of their affinity for Vincent Van Gogh's series of paintings around the subject of sunflowers. To him, it meant a
great deal of gratitude. As a feature length screenplay, many events happen within a complicated/co-dependent relationship (then again what relationship isn't, right?) - but this particular scene I think sums up what I have a love for in life; and sometimes it's only a lust, because it shifts with identity, weight - mental and physical, and

the temporary yet necessary lessons we confront when we reflect. Author Danielle Chelosky, the night we met at a prose event in which she was a reader and a presenter, told me I was born inside of a sunflower. And in the
smoking circle on the street in East Village that Friday night, there was a tall band of sunflowers - by a tree by the median, between the biking lane and the busy street. And all of the sudden I believed her. Allen Ginsberg*,
afterall, once said: we are all beautiful golden sunflowers inside. I'd heard this poem before reading it, and I'd
like to believe that was true as well, but I think altruism is dangerous; altruism from a distance, like feeding an
animal through a hole in a cage of wire or glass, is worth all tries, though it takes a different sort of effort. The
only way to form your own hypothesis on the ways people are and the way you relate to them is to conduct an experiment yourself, collect data, and keep as gentle as possible. If there is a way to be in life: it's to be gentle.

But the nature of being gentle is harsh. It's direct, and directed at a subject (or a target) and I hate the game of deciphering what's true and what isn't. What power do I even hold to do that? I don't hold any. I am speaking out of turn. But also, fuck you. I just want to feel like I belong when I clearly do not and have never done that.

Can you tell I care what you think of me? A self-conscious bitch guaranteed; and the runt chokes on her slop.

Identity and sexuality are not plagues, but expeditions. We do not have to fall into the traps of being tolerable. We can accept it, diminish it, deny it, avoid it, respond to it, or existence amongst the timeless ambiguities of being a person; don't get me wrong, there are many other options - but I'll leave those to all of us to find out. I don't want to speak out of turn again. I already did that dozens of times today. What do you inject me with? What marks we'll make on the multi-textural skin of the Earth are pending; will our shadows linger in space?

Small Cramp, Big Comfort

Don't worry, you're safe up
On the roof, I'll make sure
That you'd never, ever fall.
Starry, in the witching hour
First night on the new roof
Happy we made the move
Much is always happening
World's itchy temperament
These dragonflies sit lovely
Papa, up there somewhere
I'm happy you're next to me
We are dragons and we do
Know it, but we don't feel it
Timeless, lively, disconnect
And so, I know you for now
So stay sure of recollecting
Hot balls of ruminating time
If you sit in the sky too long
You'll burn out, and where'd
We be in the world by then?
I'm happy you're here in me
Whatever forms we will take
I'd like to sleep here but I've
Got an aversion to heat and
The sun kissing my face, yet
She knows more than we do
Sees more of us, than we do
Nurtures, pushes us more in

Collective rushes to beat an
Idea of finality we've heard
Or fade the shade of; There
Is a new goal to set. Erasure
How must we accept infinity
When what is before us is a
Projection of the light carried
By us and housed inside our
Bodies? How must we wake
And find there is nothing we
Can shake, change, shade?
We are the shade
We shake ourselves up with
Worry or poisonous thought
We'll change as we breathe
And we'll go on even when
The house falls and is built
Again.
And the stars, the jeweled
Pimples of a night's vision
Have already imploded yet
We watch their reruns and
Witness their once, young,
Impressionable innocence
They are pretty as pearls,
A single one in each joint.

Albany

Never understood, never stole, never went where the capital was, never frozen before the morning. Never going back. Never slipping on gloves made of satin. Never wishing for more than what is had. Never snapping photos in front of locals. Never scrubbing down the carpet covered with crosses. Never looking long enough to see his soul. Never correcting the time on the microwave, never through with going through what we've gone through.

Never demonstrating toys, never shrinking down, never packing last minute, never moving in on schedule. No, never pulling coins out ears, never hearing folks play in the alleys of Greenwich. Never reprising Emily Webb. Never thinking that never was definite. Never lifting a white flag with feet parallel to shoulders. Never cheeky. Never green. Never desperate. Never stuck. Never the dream itself. Never the capital of a historic state. Never that bitch in the band. Never the mind that pleads for never-minding. Never indecent. Never protected. Never a moment's worth the impression it makes. Never the tree taller than all the bugs in the forest stacked. Never an imminent misplacement of information. Never an echo past the drywalls. Never mind love in the ways needed.

It Doesn't Have to Be That Way

I went around the apartment on 144th and Broadway yesterday, on Monday, looking for Lynn's lost mail key And, by some mistake of judgment and timing, instead discovered my indecent distaste for the opposite sex.

I suppose it was always within my reach, tethered to inherited maternal instincts, yet it was lodged between the steel shoe rack, painted creme white, and the wall coated with harbor gray, thick with stifled heat and whispers from next door neighbors and shrieks from their vacuums. It was around mid-day, or what a college girl would consider middle of the day. I heard the pigeons rush off their nested ledges and the cat's feet lurching forth to see what they had done.
I always wanted a guard dog. As a past Floridian still wishing I was a Floridian, I thought to myself at the stovetop;
"I should really not be sweating this much.", and I tore half a paper towel from the roll on the wooden stake and I'd tapped it to the inner pit of my arm on both sides. I believed myself to be a descendent of Brando, some distant way I guess, and embarrassed to allow my ego to self-inflate, become callous, and annotate my existence with delusion.
Ever since my father first, well, did anything remotely influential: Playing Van Halen on the way to my practices in sports that would stereotype me as a lesbian, hand me his collection of CD's; Vincent Vega's

face and gun stuck out to me, Shark Tale, the masked man who enjoyed justifying his implementing the letter V in alliteration exercise; Or let me stay up on weekends when my mother brother and brother mother prepared to take on their worlds passively, there was an overwhelming sense of love I had for the defiance he allowed me to dare to attempt to imitate before I knew what that would imply. I was going to make my own life harder, yet in turn, know how to fight for a belief. I would clean and cook and care too much and still not enough; I became a person who could never forget or wanted to be remembered for something sort of good. Egg foo young was the lingering scent of the Family Fridge for many weeks, and I loved sitting shotgun. When I was a junior in high school, I met a boy. He scared and confused me, and I rode shotgun in his car, and I felt a familiar sense of it being inappropriate to talk as the driver drove, so I watched a film in my head and tried to remember each detail of each frame and each line of each scene with the attention and affection of a scholar and hoped that it would take me a long ways away from of the situation I found myself in. Try and true or tie. Adoration became a higher esteem than getting the practical work done; I had been accused of being half there before. In my life as of yet, I have been raped in a closet twice. I once got in trouble with grandma Sharon for digging through the compartments in her jewelry box, finding an old broach that had at one point belonged to my late grandfather, Henry, was told that I should ask before searching. I was six, and I believe at this current age, I was seeking something of his

character, as I had never met him due to his overextended heart. I believe him and I would be scarily alike, just as I am with my father, and in the way I appreciate cinema, his father. Sappy chestplate, filling that fell out the divet in my tooth, in the shower, where I awoke coated in pubescent squirt; She gave me a twisting burn on my arm on the playground and the next day a little boy on his tricycle ran over it and cut open my left heel
for fun. Little peak, peak of youth, peak of minute, peak of peaks. I am the best and worst daughter you could have asked for, and I am lost with what to do with that or how to compose myself next time we meet or even how to act.
Conversations that weren't entirely conversations, inconsequential who or what or where or why or understood or comprehended or retained or sustained; I just want to be able to fall into a sleeping state and not fully hate myself.
I found the key! I am so happy I can let my neighbors in now, only to find soon enough they planned to spend lots of effort to obtain something, which is not objectively my company. What is it with never making a strong choice that can carry water weight, reciprocate the forceful wind, expedite surrounders, surroundings, and incinerate my learned helplessness? How can I be curious and be discreet about it? The ways to acclimate for this onerous act, I have not found them, and I am overextended in believing or convincing others to believe I am utterly unloveable.

I went around the street hoping for no casted glances or unresponsive persons, and instead found shame, late, old.
Being. And I went into the alleyway, no closets here; I found a distaste for the voices prophesying these miseries.
I found the habit of fantasizing it all going well. "Ask yourself: What if it does work out?"... My mother has said.
But my mother doesn't know the way my life goes in the specific way I do, though I think it's helpful philosophy.

No

i accepted beauty as something meant not for me
to be found beautiful is fair, being seen is practice
taken to extremes in youth, a broken-toe infantry
marching to and fro in this desperate knowledge
seeking twilight's prickly potency, past summer
and the waking dreams that came and have left
i've went down with the rabbits and felt skeletal
asking to learn and receiving and, later rejecting
what i know now is to be careful of who i've met
no more will a man know me in intimate images
and i will not see it in his eye; letting it be can't
be enough. i need to erase my memory of touch
and the touch of a woman who cannot read lips
the violence of what some call love, denounce it
the transition undertaking immediate undeniable
my
burrowing bosom of nicety, sex not me else more
you chide me, and frown and draw lines, no more
i, remaining a witch in need of ease, cast my spell
only on myself - i fill my floors with wildflowers
and i've learned well that love is a made up story
conceived in a dry cave to make me feel uneasy
i have lived through thistles of belonging, despair
following through in its already lackluster promise
i bloom in my desire's grave, grow from no man's
garden when, once it seemed to be so tempestuous
it is love that i dream not of, it is an innate rebirth

Aqua Viscous

(Co-Written by S. Bruzon)

You cast your eyes on me, twisting perpendicular to the collision of our curly hairs at curl
An earring on tree
Deceased palm locust thrusting counterclockwise in fervent fertility on a brand new couch
Myth popping twister telling stories of the concepts of affections and the laws of attraction
Twin doors open
You spread a ceremonial blanket to soak spritz untidiness, I so love it when you tuck your
Index and middle finger, like sacrificed siblings, into your gaped pillow-framed oral cavity
Your hand threaded through the viscous water of the cave of our landmark geyser pitied to
Stack silver logic
Opaque miscarriage of the normal heart, troubled, bundled, wetted deep a load of laundry
In the midst of making a little money, helpless to the primitive terror, of the primitive tide
Oh, to hold a branch of you and sink further through with security in moonlit deft fashion
Platform of sticky intricacies dispensed from the eager holes of you and me and the leech
Powdered soliloquy flea contraption I love the way you taste to me, this light at this hour!

I lick at the totem

Do Unto Others

Holy ground, wildly colden broken beholden spaghetti tapestry, icy on the top of the snow coated car, despising the times thought of when seen or when the same spoken letters and formations of teeth spatially changing recreate the sound of your name. Before there is a gust I have moved my seat to the back of the classroom and aroused greater suspicions. I have acted classy, social, buttery, fly-ey, ladylike for the dustfarters, acceptable to those who practice
in missionary exclusively, and now margaritas and cheese or dogs with nothing behind their eyes but love; Babies who do not know any more or any better create vomitous in my shifting stomach. I am pissed off, softly nihilistic, and I am over the tradeoffs of being property, pride enhancer, servicing barefoot belly dancer. The supreme court
can shove the ends of their gavels, every last one of 'em, where the broken ozone's light doesn't dare shine. Every living person was once a baby and does not deserve to be killed. Didn't they teach you this in middle school along with the art of abstinence? Treat others the way they wouldn't treat you unless you had exactly what they wanted.

Pruning

Women on the beach, fabric up your ass, salt and sand. Are your teeth sliding together, like two different types of paper or is there a small piece of sand crushed from the weight of your uneven enamel canine camels? Humpback
beautiful sky. Did you buy those jeans you liked today? What did your mother say? Laugh across the universe, til' shrink, til' Boston, til' stripes, fingerpainted cactus flower and mysterious juices, ice, brussel sprouts, tomato curd around the clitoris of Mother Nature and the vines of amazement or the magazines the grasshoppers enjoy reading are no longer published - At least sold at the local corner store for grasshoppers - I saw you sleeping with them on the fourth of July and they bit at you before you noticed yourself turning red. Catchphrase of community hey, you
catch my flip flop! And give me a kiss. I don't care if the neighbors watch. Let's go outside and pierce each others ears! That'd be fun. In the woods of my life, I have found it is much easier to embrace the joy than to torture it, or puncture it with scissors, baby bag babble batch bunch bomb. Catchphrase of continuity, hey you can't do that! -It doesn't make sense with the economy and all. Women in the shallow, fabric slipping down your hips, better pull it up soon, salt and sand. The pattern of sand, send me to another dimension of sunbathed cheese, comforting froggy chicken shrimp larvae can you keep it to medium level of volume so the kids can sleep in the

sun and make fun of the old lady who didn't have kids but she loves wearing neon and decorating herself with tan lines; Want to be her friend and feed seagulls the appropriate foods that won't block their esophaguses with her. I want to see my Aunt Teresa again soon, though I've seen her before and been there before; Want to go to Cuba with the love of my life before the apocalypse is possible, though I suppose there is always a possibility of the apocalypse happening. Uh!
I can feel the truth and the truth in the truth of knowing that she feels at home in outside inside her foolish vessel, her gorgeous vessel. The sky is pale until it is not, feed the flesh and prevent the Earth's rot. Water the plants with the fruits of the ocean and understand the land better than it may understand you - Reciprocity, baby; Talk to wind and water of absolute reality, natural disorder, natural inertia of harmony, t-shirted nirvana, the curse of a Nirvana t-shirt, salt bath, bath salt, getting cashback on bananas for the lower of a pre-packaged water bottle with no name, for one, one double step, one triple step, one two three four fuck me jab me poke me with your firepoker, speak a rhyme in a world of non-rhymers and eat lesbian chocolate cake by the piers and let me know what it conjured in
your bleached denim mind. I'm coming back to standing by my forlorn teacher. We let our mouths fall open wide and unformed unrehearsed sounds spill out; Mallets, brooms, broomsticks, stickshifts, umbrellas, billings; Bridge

bridge bridge, troubled water, rocky water, wooden water. Absolute reality is and isn't anything special. How am
I going to walk around with a head full of cemented prejudices and unwavering waves of at will or to begin with?
It is the temporary lust of the divine actors and gods and practitioners and chiropractors of bacon egg and cheese.
Atlantic Beach: June Thirteenth; The polish on the toes of my left foot shade velvet - bright light vanilla purples. A bird pecks at the underwing area of itself. Hi, second bird. The liquid church crunch of the low tides tell me it makes no use or sense worrying about the way the currents are moving, energies I'll exert moving in an opposite directorial positional directional frightful time consuming shrapnel days and days worth of training in inhibition.
Young man in the turkey blue shirt to my left, blowhole your way over to the old man in the darker blue shirt on my right, half a mile West of the first catch of the day. I sit still as a median of their distances; In red, green, and turquoise. Fleets of shells giggle and pee themselves under my snowy whitey sandy feets, sensitive and insecure of flatness and my waist's desire to remove its vastness, yet if the ocean were to do that there'd be no homes for seahorses. Why did I ever go to the land of horns and taxis? I'm not pruned by the waters pressing at the surface of the world and I'm not burnt from the sun. I am no more and no less. You are south of here, and also here with

me. There does exist the genetic information of the world at some point to some extent, spread as fresh ashes do spread through the sands of the submerging and emerging at shore's breakage of mundane to what makes a man.

Dirty Yes Girl

He had me by unrequited shoulderblade.
Another he had me by the hole poked (not by me) in
those red tights I made the choice not to throw away.
Clothes, I believed them to be, were captains, dictators
even; Commanders of thought, scent, memory, etc.
The juvenile, vile bending ocean liner sunk in suggestion
of something I wasn't ready to do, yet protest is
Not such an appealing notion to a man of his breed,
speed, strength, hubris, whatever factor it had been, it
Had prevented me from preventing him.
I wish I had kept my sheers with me and not worn
clothes that required another person to zip me up, and
He zipped me up after sticking his arms through the
sleeves before mine. I wanted to kill him right there.
Medusa, medusa, do your work on his eyes the way I
wish I had. He did mine the way no man should be
Permitted legally; In any sort of essence.
I craft climates in myself to buy time, I hide razor
blades in my cheeks, in the folds of my esophagus; Yet
Prior to offenders accessing it, they must track past my
navel, bush, steering wheel, bike lock, moat, yard.
I am not so afraid to take what you have.
I swell up with heat, red light, rope burn.
I am a walking ember of suspicious origin, and I gather
you see I see you in ways a human should not be.
Turpentine, sailor tears, womanly sick, I have used my
technique to channel the slide of an eastern snake.
So you know I don't mean well anymore.

I Still Think About It

I keep waking up tonight. 8. 9. 10. 1. It's 1 now. My breath stinks and I'm still wearing yesterday's makeup. Of all things to dream about, I dreamt about sleeping in an uncomfortable-compared-to-my-current-position way. All I'd want out of life if I didn't want you would be to be proud of how I carried myself through this confusing world. O
But do the fates tell me to keep a distance from forever; You must know what I mean. I keep waking to a window reflecting the moon and the man in it. Aside from you, he is my favorite person to talk to. My neighbor across the alleyway has their light on. We're smitten with nightmares, old television, or seeing figures that aren't really there.
I roll out my foot. I blink arbitrarily, spitefully, and I touch my head and remember my hair is gone; I cut it all off.

A Woman in a Suit Made of Leather Skin

Weary life
Wearing life made of lives pre- mine own
And yet what made them high and mighty
See-through, almost yellow chipped teeth
Silkscreen
Sulking spirit for little to nothing in stock
To and fro
Fro and to
The shoes worn can inform each entrance
And removal does not constitute any exits
Plaque-coated tongue with inflamed buds
Half there, not there, half gone and baked
Slightly-off notions
For the dear panged
Rage against a trying to help type of kind

Survived, divorced from sensations of an
Apparatus for caring
I am made of blood, what do you expect
Drink the alphabet soup in kitchen sinks
There are no needs to speak about a past
Momentus
There is no need to ruin your sleep over
The action
And cannot take over the garment sewn
Embedded

Married to the absolute patterns written
That continue in the habit of
Keeping a distance to what I recognize
As detrimental to the way of all bodies
In my body
Pro and anti
Functioning

We can pluck at the pieces and separate
Evolving as
These continents have done previously.
There's enough free will left to do that.

A Sheep Among Many

The canyon floods early
The moon marmalading
The murkier, unread sunset skylight razor's edge
Affection in life a despondent vote for candidate
Familiar sister cousin mother face unfathomable

It is a matter of continuation
And coordination, what goes in front of the other
Doesn't see the butterfly, but a gratification moth
Flayed, burrowing off
The capability of bedding slow death once more
This time with company, this time with power in
The addition of bodies
The interpolated shaken ring finger, the years of
No non possessiveness
The years of the Sheep
Tight as the magic ring
Embarrassing to be alive and to give way to the
Actions of following, rolling flowers into socks
And cooking for those who do not care for fuel
To be fueled by rejection and to continue on an
Immeasurable nonlinear structure, truth telling
The moment at a moment and things going the
Other way the next day
Whomever lay beside my been-through body a
Next time, o please stay
Whomever dries their socks in the sun with me
Stay and pick flowers again with me, I haven't

Got the strength to look for you so again, again
I have lost the map of the garden with my mind
And I repeat myself as I cannot purge it enough
I haven't done much to convince these feelings
To unfollow me, I have not spayed the coats or
Flung them onto racks, embroidered even, this
Parasite of involvement
You may not remember
Or pay my mistake any
Mind, a second coming

Orchard boy is marrying early in the next year
Everyone I wanted to like me and still want to
Like me is moving on and has moved in, yet I
Traveled to another side of the country, Venus
And my mattress sinks from the weight of all,
All I have carried, and kept my life unmarried
I want a magic ring that is not yarn any longer

Thick Print

Advanced sensors enough, swan fields pressing for information, there is a light across the street of his memory
Of an older gentleman he did not introduce a family of thought to
Polyester entanglements enfold a tender teenaging prismatic soul

"Going nowhere has been on my bucket list for a very long time."

Forever uncorrupted and a flight risk, told by the face, told by one of the flaring nostrils of the face, there is an
Altruistic deception among us and it must be seeded out and bled for the ceremonial beheading of these clouds
Who have withstood and retained liquid air and mongering music

There is a light stretching through the hail, under the suffocation of heaven herself, copulating color fields that
Go unimagined and unsteady, all that must be deadened must also
Fry and share a final word with the watching, determining cluster

Of mortality here and now commencing the developing of the motionless final frame of potential innocence, a

Glaring villainy before the autonomy of gifts, or misuses of them
There is a moment of serene imprisoned sound before electricity flays his head his amygdala his moneymaker
And all that he could have been had he not absolved himself from
The category of once good, now terribly bad men in actualization
There is a moment before the scent of sweat and smoke swallows
The room in which he dies and will soon be softly extracted from

Cut crescent reddened moons standing side by side at the shoulders have created a moon shaped parentheses
We tell and are told not to look, but what happens, or more importantly - does not happen if we do not look?
For: escape, proof, thrill, tenderness, comedy, sorrow, camp, defense, offense, construction, and destruction.

American Way

What do you want as a loan now? What do you qualify for that I do not? How do you get your hair to stay clean, with this weather and everything? Did you have a kid yet? Oh, you're not pregnant? Nobody is not pregnant, no one is unfucked by the systems created and upheld and praised for being mechanical and appearing as functional
as any other method of producing a collective desire. NO! A collective benefit. Why is your life so transactional?

Who are you afraid of hurting you? Eye Roll, Drive, Crack Your Knuckles, Know This Formula, Knock My Life
Shit Off, Spit On A Bald Guy's Head While You're On A Rooftop In Long Island, Eye Roll, Turn Away From A Room With Three Mirrored Walls. I don't feel so well. Gay gummies full of magic, please save my life as I chew And Keep Your Hands and Rope Fingers and Flashed Ankles In The Jurassic Vehicle At All Times Of The Time

Don't let me operate the cash register; ever since Algebra I've been behind on how interest works or how to do a certain equation or divide anything above my weight in pounds or convert money to time. Wish we would use the metric system already, but inconsequential is the way in which we solve a problem;

as long as we terminate given issues at hand and look presentable, prepared for a plethora of publicity field tableaus; effort pays off into the gut
of the country. Serve the stranger who looks away and gawks yet doesn't acknowledge the hungry bodies and the pregnant women absolutely in need of a support system. Handcuff necklace, pig blood gloss; dying is much more expensive than it was before. What do you think of when you hear me talking like that? Calculate the cost of your well-put-together personal illusion before you go on to ridicule my disillusionment and know that I could hate you and the way you eat fast food faster than the food and with more salt and vigor than Mr. Who Is It's blood type on the annual checkup visit; the higher his cholesterol, the better he will do the company name. You are chicken. You
are synthetic synthesis. I am. She is. He is. Their children are. Some mountains are. Eyelashes are, writing is. Sure. Communicating is. Here I am coveting your mouth, how it moves around your face smugly. Water is, air is, fire is. The Earth is. Our freshly realigned, brought, partially-liquid, squeezed clumps of flesh. Our grubby implantations are and they will grow to realize they are. You'll be sat at the television, spoonfed information, understanding little of yourself, on and on wondering why, in the cardboard shrink wrapped dugout of a room at night in a night house, you feel false; you are not even a person, like the world is at the edge of ending.

Stick Bug, Name: Julia I. Charisse

Leaning ahead, looking at the end
Neither of us imagined sustaining
Built from branches, not the stem
What floated up from all red gunk
Intrepid
It was five legged and was dressed
In fine clothes, had a crooked nose
An honest temperament or reserve
Fretted
Sensations arise as if with your tide
Knocking off the misplaced weight
Granting what it was new lifted life
It's just as fond of you as you are it
Brother, sister, worthy enough, rest
In the river of the machine
Rest in the stinky dusk sowing you
Into the plains of what could I have
Been if I had just given in
Dame around dance around be pout
Loud, so proud in your alivenesses
Unprejudiced for anyone, anything
Coins behind the backs of the bulls
Boot shoe shine, oil and the solvent
Branded envelope of tongue's press
Delivered covered in dung and mud
The news

The news
I wrote you as I sitting in new shoes
Realized I was in a new phase of my
Life and listened to a city piano sing
"Do do do do do dod opdododo dod
I just want you to let me love in you
Oh historic, a prehistoric, backslide"
Landslide cutting time short, do diii
Da diii, don't stop playing this song
Play it as long as you can play it for
The holiness of the rhythm, put it to
The world that once never knew the
Way your name rhymes" - A player
Treating art as athletic sort of sport!
I think of
Greatests
I think of
The sickness of the stick bug shriek
I am nude
I am wire
I am heat
The trail treats these shoes to a show
There is no set of plays acceptable to
A court of nature and public waiting
Your inauthenticity has awakened a need in me to be authentically competitive in my work. To get ahead of myself.

Kub Lamp

I speak for myself, a self of a kind, though I'm not sure of what I am, who you are, or why the two of us ended up in this bathroom together. Do call soon watch pee this is new for me. Grate time thrash rip pancakes are the best and of the worst for me as a kid so far jarred low jacked jawed. The more I write poetry, the more I write poetry but I never speak of my love. Deal. Bonk dong bing bong tick tock touch my invisible shock whistling for the throbbing limbed instrument to come forth full of hot blood; fired up, fighting between the mirror and the sink and the angle of a head
that pulls in air to breathe with me, melt in the waxing light with me. Scrub at my lips until they bleed. Is this a new freckle?

Is this a new one? Is this a normal thing to have on my body? Is this an abnormality? Is a cute bad cute nice cute weird cute yikes cute bullshit cute orca whale eat shit and pie and combine all the things you fear into a bath and drown in it. Breaking a mirror, making an open improvisation mosaic, the trip visitor fussing over it. Lightbulbs.
Come to corner of room, I will give you a hand occupation and ride with the horses painted on the wall. Club my face in or make me pretty. Make prettiest girl ever of me in this bathtub. WET ARE HERE FOR THIS LIFE I U LOVE IT SO MUCH BAD BAD BAD FACE IN THE LIGHT. I KNOW YOU SO ALREADY KNOW WHAT

HOW'D YOU GET TO BE SO TALL cotton ball proof towel proof sink proof door knob. Proof that we be here

I Can't Give You the Address

December 10th, 2023.

I went there willingly, not knowing who the man was.
I wanted someone to talk to. I do not know why I did.

The company of someone who had ill intent is much
More manageable when that someone's your one self

His name
In practice
"To fuck" and "to fornicate" in French

Ken
I will always know who you are, asshole

It felt the least like sex, though my work
With sense memory paid off until I went
Around the corner post playing nice and
Kissing him at his door

"It's not your fault"

I wore red tights, I thought it would ward
Him off
Instead it got him off
He tried them on when I laid there unsure
Of what the next step was

I took an open container out and chugged
Walked to a station while texting my boss

I sent a smiley face to her "Goodnight!"
A month later, I would tell her I had an
Injury, but would return to work shortly.

And I found another job where I didn't
Have to interact with people as often as
I did with that one.

I went from Girl With the Pearl Earring to
Christina's World, except the illnesses had
Been there since my conception, or maybe
I had raped myself many times before that.

I just
Could not dance with my key knife the
Same

The mirror near the bath fogged twice
That night upon my coming home, and
I felt, for a moment, entirely clean of it
Freshly
Perfect
One for my mother, once for my father
One will not know for a humor of time

I wanted a man in my life to apologize
For the wrongdoings of the other men
That didn't mean to be rough or offend

But they were and they did and I don't
Like living with it
That man, that stranger, that fashioned
Language barrier, hard bodied did lied
Shock is not my symptom sustained, I
Am not at all surprised that night gave
Way to some loneliness bursting from
Pipe
Eager, kind of disturbingly childliked
Need to call the superintendent, but I
Am worried there'll be no hearing us

"Evacuate the premises immediately"

There is no such thing as purity close
There is no revenge I could take, nor
Would I want to enact that terror, for
What would become of me after that

What fuse would make lack of peace
Light and detonate in a fit of passion
What people would want me to shut
My fucking mouth, or keep quiet for
The simple joys of appearing purely
Here and there and untouched by an
Unwell flickering stairwell, hundred
Plus a hundred plus a thousand mile
Trek from the first person I told it to

I didn't wear lipstick on that evening
It was the first time I'd fucked sober

I remember, the first man inside me
Didn't kiss me
Did I do anything about the offense?
No, I did not tell the authorities
I had some grand education that day

And each day is another education
And miseducation
Each day I find what to love and to
Avoid.

And I see that continuing only if I
Am caught sleeping or being anal,
Open, obvious, grateful, or lustful

I performed for my rapist, but I'd
Walked through the rain, to home
Where I wasn't only this mistake.

In the Cinematic Midnightly Mind

I'm writing you on my deathbed, deadcot, deadland; our
Citizens are deadened, deadening each other in repetition
Do not look only to pretty or undecided things for breath
Do not rely on being told what to do by your fellow man
Thought it is useful though it briefly dilutes the madness
Just out into dreaming spare why yonder nothing gleams
Were there ever such horrifically bleeding times as these

There is no savior satiating the terrorism of abundances
There is incomprehensible dissonance, I'm sure you see
In the back of your mind as you sleep for four hours off
And on
Glittering silvery prenuptials of Nirvana sleeping ahead

The rush of the world to come, horn echo triumphs here
Whirling bashful naked withstanding structures, subtext
Here we go hoping in the inevitable middle of midnight
Throttled by intentions and the intent of prismatic plays
If I were to tell you of my love equal to my terror, what
Would you hold by my face, what visions could waft in
Supposing forces without formidable bodies performed

Here we go singing mindful and sorrowful songs again

A fresh reel loaded in, a budget of transactional loving
Liquified craft stimulated lacrimal gland and cosmosis
Delegating a drowsing, commencing a noble buoyancy

Sheets of Rain

Let the ocean take me into her soft arms, rippled and
wrinkled from the stretching of her time on this Earth
Maps, digital or in print, do not indicate the path to
Venus Beach between my trigonometrical needy knees
Her place in the world is the most vital one, calmly
assuming the position of general, stoic until an ambush
Of blush and the enthusiasm of parting the sea within
and outside herself, one with herself; she the element
of how things are.
I say to Venus on
Each night breath
"Teach me to fear little, to be embarrassed by little, to
question little when I'm called to interpret beauty as
Written and witnessed by a god, an entity, and identity
with which would have been given a written name"
But we're young
And we're older
Than the young,
And there were a million that practiced love with the
utmost effort and effaced unrepressed feminine age
Before we were born, and they learned over time how to
hold each other and how to dress to satisfaction

Joan of Arc of the south; thorough aventurine; raisined,
seasoned, and unsimple in a blonde transparency
Wine drunk, bows in hair, loving completely, soaking up
the sunshines of your smile being in attendance

Let an ocean of listening heal and surf the triangles of sadness breezing while freeing ourselves of haunt.

What It Means to Place Trust and Wait to Find Out

When will I learn to forgive fully, or wholly, here?
Fully swarmed in arm, fully discerned, fully home
With what home means; to be at home, to come a
Long ways, and return, and to feel a full salvation
Of the exhausted, done before, clamped accidents
No one else remembers; they gift me restlessness
Quiet and swole as the ordained misaligned, fake
And organic, and baked, and cooked, and blazed,
Trimestered, festered, craved, insolent, behavior
Unrehearsed, italicized state of arriving to home
Long awaited, chained, intensely tethered to the
Wicker, and woolen warmth, or unbearable heat
No place meeting that criteria, it seems, I know.
I have read of domesticity within the individual

To tell what I do with the gifts of a ripened day
With a face familiar and body unexpeditioned
Do I desire or am I someone fully conditioned?
Tested out of many troubling things, in Florida
Passed by a single point, over and over against
The barrier of some unruly, heavenly, hellbent
Undisclosed, culpable, feathered, tactfully tied
All-knowing knob, reciting as I read fine print
And you current, you are not, were never mine
Nestled in cities between idealized and adored
Bodies, and tenements, and pregnancy worries

Ditka's Ball

Attention, keep the faucet on, Joes, flooding flooding the tub's rim, her eyes baking, melting, sweating, precipitation of the weakling who does not know how to ask for better treatment; abandon a bathroom bottled when the request is not only rejected, but receptive as little as possible as little as little possible, of all that -
pasted applied white gelatin
patted flatly, she's in the same room as two exceptional dancers by her standards - actually the school's standards bi
per usual, a girl from Portugal has pretty canines; olfactory aid, ro, bean toast, forgetaboutthefailuresinclasslastweek

Fleece men, these geese men removing their noses when taking in new patients at the infirmary, by the beach, and they often are seen removing a sliver of the prefrontal cortex, a primitive penetration of the mind, a forced rubbing and touching of the cartilage rind, intimacy of the senseless under the stern voyeurism of an American government
cinnamon, the key to financial safety in a rut such as this one's to give them a piece of your individualistic identity
bail me out babe limoncello exploitation of the dance we find ourselves at having received and read no invitations haven't the resolve for such trespassing carnal knowledge down to the rotten science of it, watching the

clock, got ants and plants and transplants nowhere near
that emotion or emotional notion, a fastened excitation
prompts back to be in order frustrated with the time
and place dip my face in the silver facade of virginity
processed, mine mine,
this tumescence is mine all mine after all this time you
can't take that from me this time not my nose this time,
red
my tumescence is mine, all mine, only mine, after all
hungry ladder only sketching the silhouette of a deep
dream
enraged with the erasure that's brewing, there's no way
I can do this procedure on my own, thumbtack plush
days
educating this time, the depth of your seniority, knowing
better, separate from forever, you dog, argument, spliced
into the words funneled into your mouth, drop off, soft
day, firm day, turn the page, turn the page, keep
learning a
lesson on what will work to get you out of this and what
will not in the vaporized falling off my removal of grade

Learn to be funny, learn to be sex on legs, to smile
more, learn how to show and not tell. Be good and don't
show

That is the Girl

Knowing when to draw the line, quite grown up her way, from picking dandelions to managing, organizing, fixing every single detail before she must force herself to rest. And even then it's a turbulent rest. It's incorrect rest, it's a shoehorned burnt popcorn rest. She'll break your heart before she means to. She'll horn you into her shoe, and you sit in her kitchen, see her birthday balloon sitting next to your head, floating still but at a loss for air. She's stopped celebrating that day, as that day is only one day and that particular day is just another day to her and today is a day and the next day to come will be a day and when she wakes up early in the morning and boils an egg and cuts it in half and fixes her coffee and brushes through her tangled hair and makes a wish in the mirror and practices how to ask for a promotion and fastens her jacket and takes her bag off the hook by the door and shuts the door and locks the door and leaves for her car and gets in the car and starts the engine it'll be a day. And she'll realize she forgot about brushing her teeth. And she'll be at least four minutes late for work that particular day because the traffic is especially packed on Tuesdays. And she will always prefer Thursday if the rules of engagement forbid preferring Friday. And she'll think about Carrie Mae Weems in the office and imagine the composition and lighting setup of her own private kitchen table series. And she'll feel sure she can take on today's assignment as her colleagues tap

her shoulder and hand her a file. And she doesn't feel
quite sure how to respond to their persistent questions,
day
in and day out. And she'll check the file and sit up and
prepare her equipment and plan to go to the scene. And
a wind will whisper through the doors and she'll receive
the message that another missing girl was discovered
and
she's gotta pay a visit today. And this particular day,
she'll be menstruating, so she'll be in tune with herself,
and maybe she'll be a little on edge because of that and
a myriad of things. And she'll start up the car, but she'll
take
a moment to breathe. And she'll need to get some water.
She'll forget again about a basic necessity. She'll guess
she can wait. She'll play Meredith Brooks in the car and
think about a girl she loved when she was the same age
as the girl on file. She'll arrive at the scene, feeling
unkempt but hiding it, and she'll listen to the symphony
of a forest floor filled with rustling leaves. And she'll
take her camera with her. She'll remember that detail.
And she
will approach a school of investigators and show them
her badge and they'll nod their heads and let her
through.
And she'll be through. And she'll take a moment to
consider what she is to do when she stands within steps
of a freshly dug up college girl. And a coroner will ask
her to begin taking photographs. And she'll begin a
series of photographs. And she'll see, as two

investigators pry at the girl's skirt with a professional twig, that this girl has
also had her menses. She'll remember that detail. And she'll photograph her fingernails coated and stuffed with Ohio soil. And she'll photograph the maggot ballet in the hair on the girl's head. And she'll photograph the pair of shoes nearby, much too slim in width to fit the girl. And she'll press one of the coroners for information, and they will say it's too soon to know for sure if it was foul play or not. And she'll photograph the lacerations, and the rashes, and the rotted bits, and the missing teeth, and the broken wrists, both of them broken bones, and she
will arrive home later that day and not eat dinner and remember those details. And she will get to bed early, and she'll turn the leaf light projector on and lay in a vision of a tranquil forest and fail to forget the girl she missed.

The detail in the day. The dental records of day. The daytal dencords of the yad. The record skips, and spins on.

I Wish I Had An Excuse

As to why I can't quite commit to my life
I feel the billowing need to explain action

And I wonder without a rest as to why for
Why now, I'm happy for you, gracious as
You, depleted and domesticated by doubt

Little do you know my drive to shout out
And cry out and ask "Why don't you love
Me" and remove coherent denial for spite
As if I might be finally good at something
Get some new skill to do at dinner parties
Drums of mass strip away that swift rider
Bold sharpness into my smirking sternum

I feel sick all the time, I really do feel so
Sick from all the lime rhymes squeezing
By in my mind cross those plains a pain,
Like no other, like whales under my feet
Like skydiving and waiting to pull chute
Like a buttondown unbuttoned and open

Outed

As to how I got into my aunt's burnt attic
How
Dressed in lasting ash, dancing laps into
The far corner checking its own pulsing

Pulse Denver dad wishing bet then best
But bested by the truest bestest boykind
I'm graduating from an academy of day
Thankfully, it's been long enough, and I
Suck with making respectable decisions

What sober words I have said to friends
I do not know what they are
I couldn't spell them out if you gave me
A pencil and tied me
To a chair or threatened my flipflop life
I wish I could give you a proper excuse
A brilliant one
I really wish I could
I wish I'd the ambition to do that to you

US:

RAINN - National Sexual Assault Hotline - 800.656.4673 - rainn.org

S.A.F.E. Alternatives (Self-Abuse Finally Ends) self-harm helpline: 800-DONT CUT
(800-366-8288)

Crisis Support Services national helpline: 800-273-8255

Teen Line for youth in need of support: 800-852-8336

UK:

Rape Crisis National Telephone Helpline in England and Wales: 0808 802 9999

Rape Crisis Scotland helpline: 08088 01 03 02

SupportLine for emotional support on any issue: 01708 765200

Self Injury Support Helpline for women: 0808 800 8088

SOUTH AFRICA:

The Gender-Based Violence Command Centre (GBVCC) Emergency Line: 0800 428 428

Akeso 24 hour emergency contact: 0861 435 787

NEW ZEALAND:

Lifeline 24/7 Helpline: 0800 543 354

Women's Refuge Crisisline: 0800 733 843 (0800 REFUGE)

OUTLine NZ: 0800 688 5463 (OUTLINE)

PHILIPPINES:

Tawag Paglaum - Centro Bisaya 24/7 crisis intervention and suicide prevention hotline:
Smart/Sun: 0939-9375433, 0939-9365433,
Globe/TM: 0927-6541629

In Touch Philippines free and anonymous 24/7 crisis line: +63 2 8893 7603, +63 917 800 1123, or +63 922 893 8944

IRELAND:

Rape Crisis Help Ireland 24 Hour Helpline: 1800 778888

Women's Aid 24hr National Freephone Helpline: 1800 341 900

LGBT Ireland helpline: 1890 929 539

Aware Depression & Bipolar Disorder Support: Freephone 1800 80 48 48

AUSTRALIA:

Suicide Call Back Service: 1300 659 467

Men's Referral Service advice for men worried about their behavior: 1300 766 491

QLife LGBTQ+ support helpline: 1800 184 527

Sane Australia counseling support for mental health issues: 1800 187 263

CANADA:

WAVAW rape crisis centre national crisis and info line: 1-877-392-7583

Klinic Sexual Assault Line: 204-786-8631 or 1-888-292-7565

Crisis Services Canada Suicide Prevention Service: 1-833-456-4566

LGBT Youthline: 1-800-268-9688 or text 647-694-4275

Trans Lifeline peer support service: 1-877-330-6366

PFLAG LGBTQ+ peer-to-peer support: 1-888-530-6777

Hope for Wellness 24/7 Help Line mental health counselling and crisis intervention for all Indigenous peoples across Canada: 1-855-242-3310

INDIA:

Jeevan Aastha Helpline for mental health counseling: 1800 233 3330

1Life 24-7 suicide prevention and crisis support: 7893078930

NCW Women's HelpLine: 7827-170-170

SNEHA Crisis Helpline for women and children: 98330 52684 or 91675 35765

Queerythm helpline for LGBTIQ community: +91 9747811406

Naz Foundation for Lesbian and Women Sexuality Support: +91 11 41325042 or +91 11 40793157/58

Voice that Cares Psychosocial First Aid (PSFA) Helpline: 8448-8448-45

Jordan Marcum (she/they) is an actor, poet, and student based in Brooklyn, NY. A lover of theatre, all things cinematic, crochet, and animals. Jordan is a team member at NOVA LitMag, an online resource bringing intergenerational writing and artwork to all who are seeking inspiration and movement. Recent film projects: Fly Me to the Moon (Dir. Greg Berlanti), Somebody to Love (Dir. Christopher Frentzel, Tubi & Prime Video), and STREAM (Dir. Yami, YouTube) She has also written, directed, and shot two short films out on YouTube: Burlap Doll and Delusion Baklava.
In Spring 2025, Jordan will be a graduate of the New York Conservatory for Dramatic Arts (Film & TV)
Jordan would like to thank you for reading, their mother and father for all of their love,
and all poets who have shared their work in any degree through this shared life. May we endure, celebrate, reconfigure, and adapt.
Thank you to Adam for the belief, time, and care through this creative process.
Finally, thank you to Alfie, the one true boss.

RELEASED BY DARK THIRTY POETRY

ANTHOLOGY ONE
THIS ISN'T WHY WE'RE HERE
MORTAL BEINGS
POEMS THAT WERE WRITTEN ON TRAINS BUT WEREN'T WRITTEN ABOUT TRAINS
CLOSING SHIFT DREAMS
DESIRE
ANIMATE
THESEUS AND I
I DON'T HAVE THE WORDS FOR THIS
CONVERSATIONS BETWEEN THE SUN AND THE MOON
SLUT POP
JADED
I'VE BIRTHED AN IDEA OF YOU
BRUISES
CITY GOTHIC
LONG DIVISION
SAY HER NAME
LUMIN
VESTIGES
FALLING IN LOVE LOST
JUGGERNAUT
STIRRING TO LIFE
FORGOTTEN FRAGMENTS OF TIME
THIS BOOK IS NOT ABOUT JAPAN
BEYOND THE DOORS OF A LAST BREATH
CORPORATE
JANE F*CKING EYRE
THE SNAKE EATS ITSELF
THE MOON AND HER CRATERS
NOCTURNAL
BREWING ANXIETEA
FLAT FRONT

www.ingramcontent.com/pod-product-compliance
Lightning Source LLC
Chambersburg PA
CBHW071145090426

42736CB00012B/2241